Time and Clocks

Words by Herta S. Breiter

formerly Research Chemist
University of Illinois

Raintree Childrens Books

Milwaukee • Toronto • Melbourne • London

Library of Congress Number: 77-19007

        5 6 7 8 9 0 85 84 83

Printed and bound in the United States of America.

Library of Congress Cataloging in Publication Data

Breiter, Herta S.
   Time and clocks.

   (Read about)
   Bibliography: p.
   Includes index.
   SUMMARY: Discusses several concepts of time
and various timekeeping devices.
      1. Time — Juvenile literature. 2. Clocks and
watches — Juvenile literature. [1. Time.
2. Clocks and watches] I. Title.
QB209.5.M65 529'.7 77-19007
ISBN 0-8393-0088-3 lib. bdg.

Time and Clocks

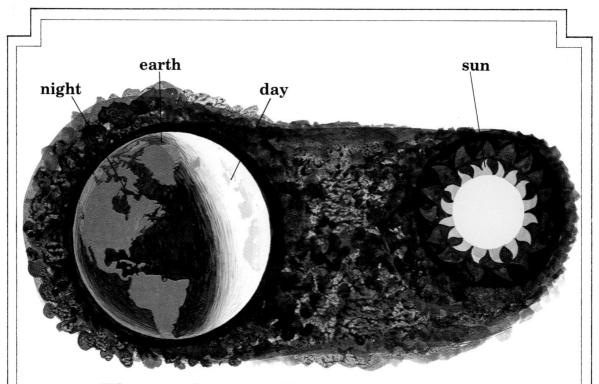

night   earth   day   sun

The earth spins like a top. It never stops spinning. It takes the earth one day to turn all the way around. The turning of the earth gives us day and night. The part of the earth that faces the sun has daytime. As the earth spins, it turns away from the sun's light. When the earth turns far enough, light cannot reach that part of the earth. Then it is night. When that part of the earth comes all the way around, the light can reach it again. Then it is day.

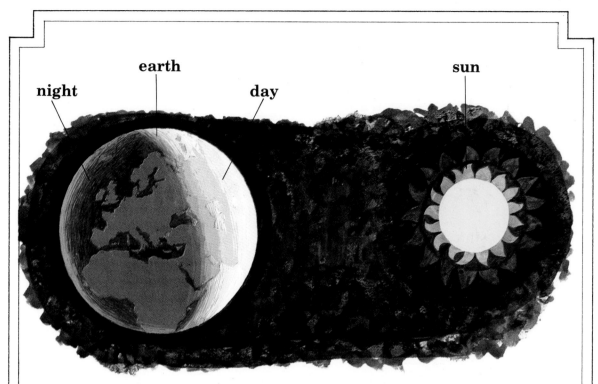

night   earth   day   sun

A day has two parts. They are called A.M. and P.M. Each part is twelve hours long. P.M. time starts at noon. Noon is twelve o'clock in the daytime. P.M. time lasts until midnight. Midnight is twelve o'clock in the night. A.M. time starts at midnight. A.M. time lasts until noon the next day.

Spin a globe of the earth as you shine a flashlight on it. Watch day and night begin on the globe where you live.

shadow

Long ago people watched the sun change its place in the sky. They saw that shadows also changed. They could tell how much time had passed by looking at the way shadows changed. They used an object that made the shadow as a clock. Some shadow clocks had a post in the middle. The shadow moved in a circle as the day went on. Some shadow clocks are called sundials.

Try this little test. Use the shadow of a flagpole or a tall tree. Watch how the shadow moves as the sun changes its place in the sky. Every hour mark where the shadow is.

sundial

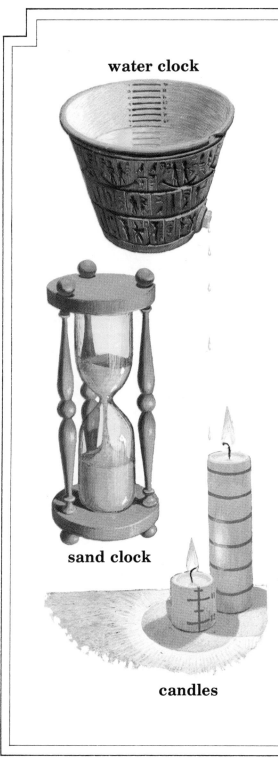

water clock

sand clock

candles

Shadow clocks worked only when the sun was shining. So people made other clocks.

The water clock dripped water out of a bowl. The water level inside the bowl showed how much time had passed.

In sand clocks, grains of sand fell through a hole. When all the sand had fallen, the clock was turned upside down to start timing again.

Some people used candles with marks. It took an hour for the candle to burn down to a mark.

jack

bell

jack

Many people tried to make new kinds of clocks. One kind of clock had bells. The bells rang every hour. People who heard the bells knew what time it was. Some bell clocks had toy men who rang the bells. These toy men were called jacks.

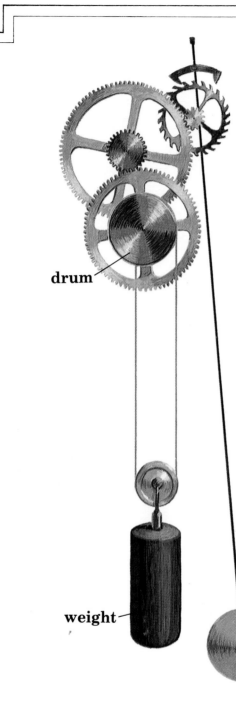

drum

weight

pendulum

Many early clocks worked because they had a pendulum. A pendulum swings from side to side.

A heavy weight made the pendulum swing. As the weight lowered slowly, it made a small, round drum turn. The drum turned wheels that made the pendulum swing.

The pendulum had a small bar across the top. The bar moved when the pendulum moved. The bar was attached to the hands of the clock. When the bar moved, the hands of the clock also moved. The position of the hands showed what time it was.

The best-known pendulum clocks are called grandfather clocks.

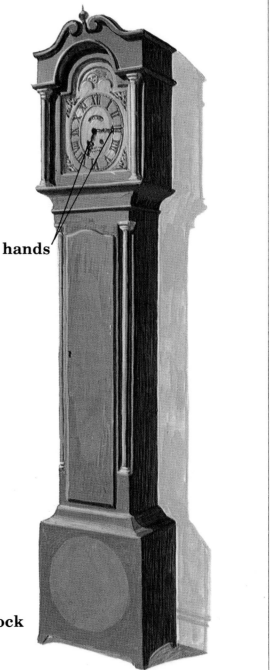

hands

grandfather clock

minutes

The numbers on the face of a clock go from one to twelve. The little hand of a clock points to the hour. The big hand points to the minutes. There are sixty minutes in an hour. The hands go around the way the arrow points. In ten minutes, the big hand will be on two. In sixty minutes, the little hand will point to five.

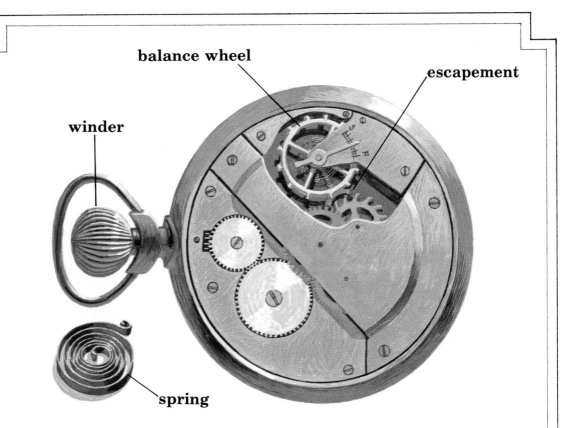

balance wheel

escapement

winder

spring

The picture shows the inside of a watch. It works by a spring made of wire. To make the watch go, you wind the spring. Then the spring slowly unwinds and turns a balance wheel. A balance wheel works like a pendulum. It moves steadily, always at the same speed. The balance wheel moves an escapement. The escapement moves the hands of the watch.

alarm clock

electric clock

watch

People need to know what time it is. People wear watches so they will always know the time. People also use alarm clocks. These clocks ring a bell to wake people up.

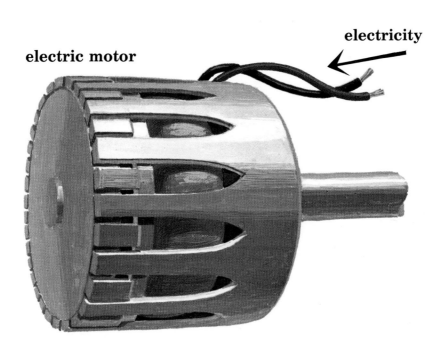

electricity

electric motor

Electric clocks do not need winding. They run as long as electricity flows into them. Electricity runs a small electric motor. The electric motor takes the place of the windup spring.

The time is 28 minutes after twelve. This clock has no hands. It tells the hours and minutes in numbers. It is called a digital clock.

This is a special clock that sailors use. It is called a chronometer. It keeps time very accurately.

chronometer

But these two clocks are even more accurate. They are used by scientists. The atomic clock uses the fast movement, or vibration, of atoms. Atoms are tiny bits of material.

The quartz-crystal clock uses small pieces of a mineral called quartz. Electricity makes the quartz vibrate quickly. Scientists use these clocks in their work.

atomic clock

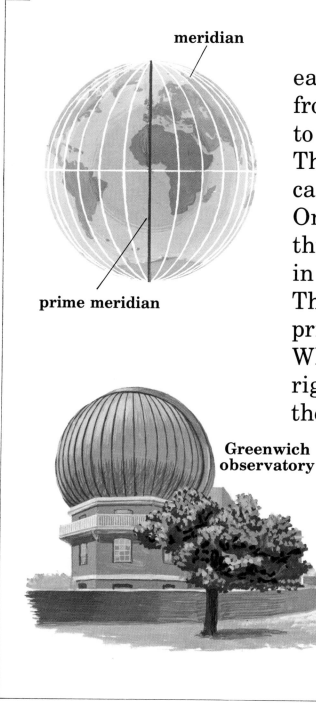

meridian

prime meridian

Greenwich observatory

On a map of the earth there are lines from the North Pole to the South Pole. These lines are called meridians. One of the lines goes through Greenwich in London, England. This is called the prime meridian. When the sun is right over this line, the time is noon.

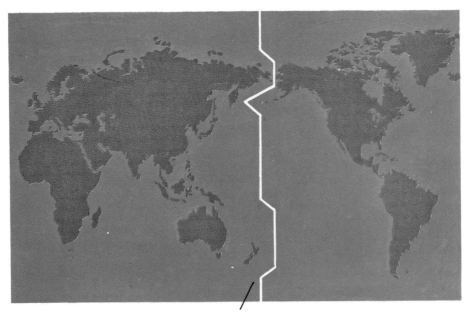

Tuesday   **international date line**   **Monday**

When it is noon at Greenwich, it is midnight halfway around the world. The meridian there is called the international date line. It is there that the day begins. On the east side of this line, at midnight, it is Monday. But on the west side, it is Tuesday.

JANUARY						
S	M	T	W	T	F	S
1	2	3	4	5	6	7
8	9	10	11	12	13	14
15	16	17	18	19	20	21
22	23	24	25	26	27	28
29	30	31				

FEBRUARY						
S	M	T	W	T	F	S
			1	2	3	4
5	6	7	8	9	10	11
12	13	14	15	16	17	18
19	20	21	22	23	24	25
26	27	28				

MARCH						
S	M	T	W	T	F	S
			1	2	3	4
5	6	7	8	9	10	11
12	13	14	15	16	17	18
19	20	21	22	23	24	25
26	27	28	29	30	31	

APRIL						
S	M	T	W	T	F	S
						1
2	3	4	5	6	7	8
9	10	11	12	13	14	15
16	17	18	19	20	21	22
23/30	24	25	26	27	28	29

MAY						
S	M	T	W	T	F	S
	1	2	3	4	5	6
7	8	9	10	11	12	13
14	15	16	17	18	19	20
21	22	23	24	25	26	27
28	29	30	31			

JUNE						
S	M	T	W	T	F	S
				1	2	3
4	5	6	7	8	9	10
11	12	13	14	15	16	17
18	19	20	21	22	23	24
25	26	27	28	29	30	

JULY						
S	M	T	W	T	F	S
						1
2	3	4	5	6	7	8
9	10	11	12	13	14	15
16	17	18	19	20	21	22
23/30	24/31	25	26	27	28	29

AUGUST						
S	M	T	W	T	F	S
		1	2	3	4	5
6	7	8	9	10	11	12
13	14	15	16	17	18	19
20	21	22	23	24	25	26
27	28	29	30	31		

SEPTEMBER						
S	M	T	W	T	F	S
					1	2
3	4	5	6	7	8	9
10	11	12	13	14	15	16
17	18	19	20	21	22	23
24	25	26	27	28	29	30

OCTOBER						
S	M	T	W	T	F	S
1	2	3	4	5	6	7
8	9	10	11	12	13	14
15	16	17	18	19	20	21
22	23	24	25	26	27	28
29	30	31				

NOVEMBER						
S	M	T	W	T	F	S
			1	2	3	4
5	6	7	8	9	10	11
12	13	14	15	16	17	18
19	20	21	22	23	24	25
26	27	28	29	30		

DECEMBER						
S	M	T	W	T	F	S
					1	2
3	4	5	6	7	8	9
10	11	12	13	14	15	16
17	18	19	20	21	22	23
24/31	25	26	27	28	29	30

Calendars show us the time in days, weeks, and months. Each week has seven days. Each month has four weeks and some extra days. There are twelve months in each year. Long ago, the Romans worked out the calendar. They gave names to the twelve months.

The length of the month is based on how long the moon takes to go around the earth. Seven of the months have 31 days each. Four of the months have 30 days each. February has 28 days, except in leap year. Then it has 29 days.

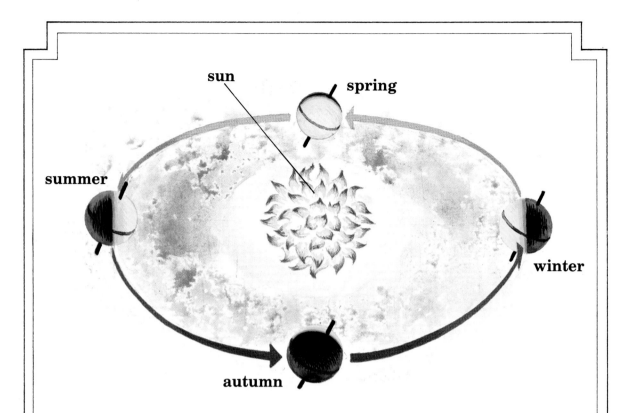

The earth travels around the sun once every 365 days. This length of time is a year. During some months of the year, the top half of the earth leans toward the sun. When this happens, it is summer on that part of the earth. It is winter on that part when it leans away from the sun.

spring

summer

autumn

winter

Actually, the earth takes a bit more than 365 days to go around the sun. So every fourth year we add an extra day to the month of February to correct the calendar. This year is called leap year.

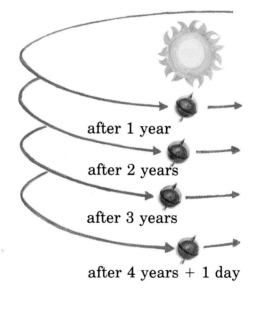

after 1 year

after 2 years

after 3 years

after 4 years + 1 day

Animals and plants do not need clocks and calendars to know time.

Swallows and other birds always know when it is nearly winter. They know when to fly south to the warmer places.

Some plants, such as the daisy, open their flowers only during the daytime. Others, such as the cereus, open only at night.

daisy

cereus

oyster

Oysters open and close their shells as the tide changes. They do this even if they are not near the sea.

squirrel

Squirrels know when to gather extra food and store it for the long winter.

And some plants know how the weather will change many hours before it happens.

potato plant

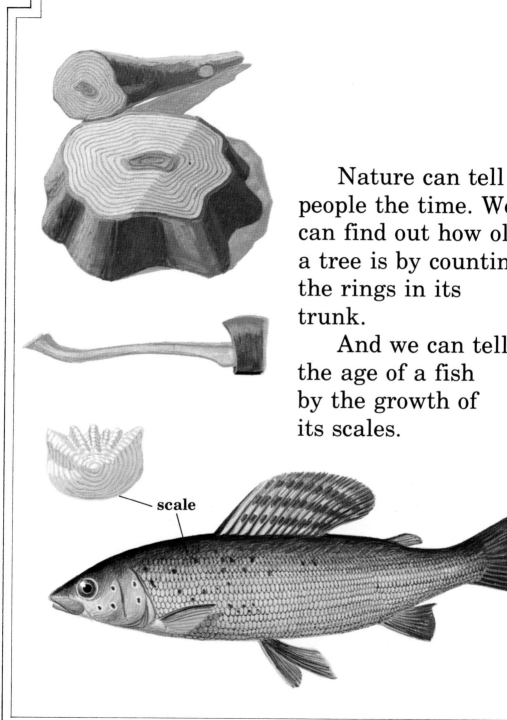

Nature can tell people the time. We can find out how old a tree is by counting the rings in its trunk.

And we can tell the age of a fish by the growth of its scales.

scale

Deep under the ground we can find the shapes of things that lived long ago. The shapes are pressed into rocks. They are called fossils. The age of the rock in which fossils are found can tell us how long ago different animals and plants lived.

dragonfly

fern

snail

fish

coral

Fossils

There is a special way to tell how long ago plants and animals lived. This is called carbon dating. All living things have atoms of carbon in their bodies. There are two different kinds of carbon. When living things die, the carbon slowly changes. Scientists know how long one kind of carbon takes to change to the other kind. They see how much carbon has changed in a plant or animal. Then they can tell how old it is.

living things today	
Cenozoic period	
Mesozoic period	
Paleozoic period	

past present future

When something is happening now, it is in the present. When something has already happened, we say it is past. In the past, you were a baby. When something will happen later, we say it is in the future. In the future, you will be grown up.

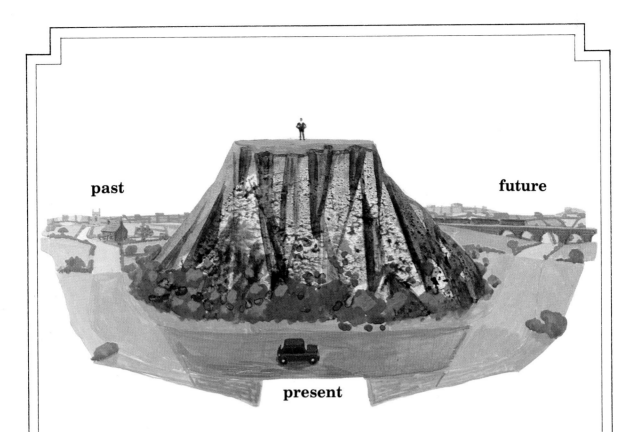

past

future

present

But time can depend on who and where
you are. People travel through a town in a
car. The town is in the past for them. The
bridge ahead of them is in their future.
But someone on top of the hill can see the
bridge and the car and the town all at once.
So they are all in the present for that person.

Time is measured by things that move. The turning of the earth measures a day. But moving things are also measured by time. The speed of a car is measured by the number of miles or kilometers it will travel in an hour. If it takes a car an hour to go 50 miles, we say its speed is 50 miles per hour.

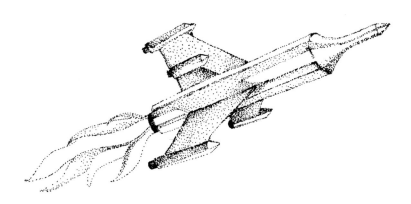

Light is the fastest thing we know. It travels millions of miles in a minute. A light-year is how far light travels in one year. Light-years are used to measure how far away stars are. Stars are many light-years from the earth. Even a very fast rocket would take many, many years to reach a star.

World Time Zones

The earth is divided into 24 standard time zones. Each zone differs from the one before by one hour. The starting point is in England. As you travel east, each zone is one hour later.

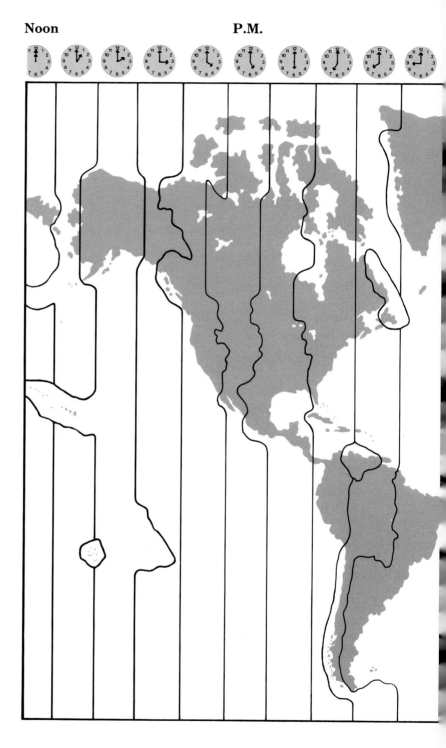

34

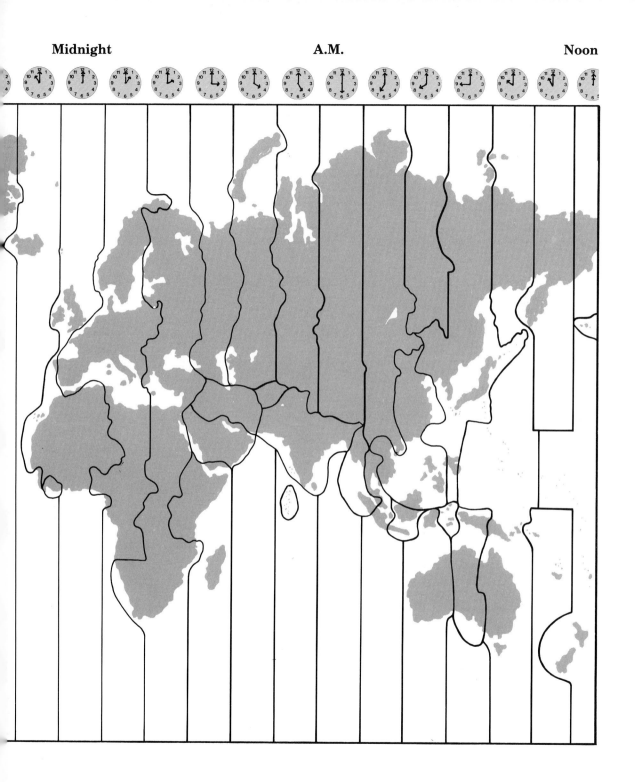

The Metric System

In the United States, things are measured in inches, pounds, quarts, and so on. Most countries of the world use centimeters, kilograms, and liters for these things. The United States uses the American system to measure things. Most other countries use the metric system. By 1985, the United States will be using the metric system, too.

In some books, you will see two systems of measurement. For example, you might see a sentence like this: "That bicycle wheel is 27 inches (69 centimeters) across." When all countries have changed to the metric system, inches will not be used any more. But until then, you may sometimes have to change measurements from one system to the other. The chart on the next page will help you.

All you have to do is multiply the unit of measurement in Column 1 by the number in Column 2. That gives you the unit in Column 3.

Suppose you want to change 5 inches to centimeters. First, find inches in Column 1. Next, multiply 5 times 2.54. You get 12.7. So, 5 inches is 12.7 centimeters.

Column 1	Column 2	Column 3
THIS UNIT OF MEASUREMENT	TIMES THIS NUMBER	GIVES THIS UNIT OF MEASUREMENT
inches	2.54	centimeters
feet	30.	centimeters
feet	.3	meters
yards	.9	meters
miles	1.6	kilometers
ounces	28.	grams
pounds	.45	kilograms
fluid ounces	.03	liters
pints	.47	liters
quarts	.95	liters
gallons	3.8	liters
centimeters	.4	inches
meters	1.1	yards
kilometers	.6	miles
grams	.035	ounces
kilograms	2.2	pounds
liters	33.8	fluid ounces
liters	2.1	pints
liters	1.06	quarts
liters	.26	gallons

Where to Read About
Time and Clocks

Pronunciation Key

a	a as in **cat, bad**
ā	a as in **able**, ai as in **train**, ay as in **play**
ä	a as in **father, car**, o as in **cot**
e	e as in **bend, yet**
ē	e as in **me**, ee as in **feel**, ea as in **beat**, ie as in **piece**, y as in **heavy**
i	i as in **in, pig**, e as in **pocket**
ī	i as in **ice, time**, ie as in **tie**, y as in **my**
o	o as in **top**, a as in **watch**
ō	o as in **old**, oa as in **goat**, ow as in **slow**, oe as in **toe**
ô	o as in **cloth**, au as in **caught**, aw as in **paw**, a as in **all**
oo	oo as in **good**, u as in **put**
o͞o	oo as in **tool**, ue as in **blue**
oi	oi as in **oil**, oy as in **toy**
ou	ou as in **out**, ow as in **plow**
u	u as in **up, gun**, o as in **other**
ur	ur as in **fur**, er as in **person**, ir as in **bird**, or as in **work**
yo͞o	u as in **use**, ew as in **few**
ə	a as in **again**, e as in **broken**, i as in **pencil**, o as in **attention**, u as in **surprise**
ch	ch as in **such**
ng	ng as in **sing**
sh	sh as in **shell, wish**
th	th as in **three, bath**
<u>th</u>	th as in **that, together**

GLOSSARY

These words are defined the way they are used in this book

A.M. (ā em) the time between midnight and noon

alarm clock (ə lärm′ kläk) a clock that can be set to make a noise at a certain time

atom (at′ əm) the smallest particle of an element

atomic clock (ə täm′ ik kläk′) a clock that is run by vibrating atoms

balance wheel (bal′ əns hwēl′) in a watch, a wheel that turns at a steady speed and moves the escapement, which moves the hands

calendar (kal′ ən dər) a device that shows time in days, weeks, and months

carbon dating (kär′ bən dāt′ ing) a way to tell how old something is by seeing how much carbon is in it

chronometer (krə näm′ ət ər) a special clock that keeps very accurate time

day (dā) the time it takes for the earth to spin around once

digital clock (dij′ ət əl klä̈k′) a clock that has changing numerals rather than hands

electric clock (i lek′ trik klä̈k′) a clock that is run by an electric motor

electricity (i lek tris′ ə tē) energy that is made by flowing electrons

escapement (əs kāp′ mənt) the part of a watch that moves the hands

fossil (fäs′ əl) the shape of a thing that was pressed into a rock many, many years ago

future (fyo͞o′ chər) the time when something will happen

globe (glōb) a ball that has a map of the world on it

grandfather clock (grand′ fä<u>th</u> ər klä̈k′) a large clock that is run by a pendulum

hour (äuər) a unit of time that has 60 minutes

international date line (in tər nash′ ən əl dāt′ līn) the meridian halfway around the world from the prime meridian. At midnight, it is Monday on the east side of the line, and it is Tuesday on the west side.

jack (jak) the toy man that rings the bells in a bell clock

leap year (lēp′ yir) the year when one day is added to February in order to correct the calendar

light-year (līt′ yir) the distance light travels in one year. Light-years are used to measure the distances between planets or stars.

meridian (mə rid′ ē ən) on a map, a line that runs from the North Pole to the South Pole

minute (min′ ət) a unit of time that has 60 seconds

month (munth) a unit of time measured

by how long it takes the moon to go
around the earth

night (nīt) the time when a place is
turned away from the sun

P.M. (pē em) the time between noon
and midnight

past (past) the time when something has
already happened

pendulum (pen′ jə ləm) an object that
makes clock hands move by swinging
from side to side

present (prez′ ənt) the time when
something is happening now

prime meridian (prīm′ mə rid′ ē ən)
the meridian that runs through
Greenwich, London. When the sun
is over the prime meridian it is noon.

quartz (kwôrts) a mineral that is made
up of many six-sided crystals

quartz-crystal clock (kwôrts′ kris′ təl
kläk′) a clock that is run by vibrating
quartz crystals

sand clock (sand′ kläk) a clock that tells time by the amount of sand that has passed through a hole in the middle of the clock

second (sek′ ənd) the smallest unit of time on most clocks

shadow clock (shad′ ō kläk′) a clock with a post in its middle whose shadow moves as the sun moves

speed (spēd) how fast something is moving

summer (sum′ər) the time of year when the earth leans toward the sun

sundial (sun′ dīl) a kind of shadow clock

vibrate (vī′ brāt) to move back and forth, usually rapidly

watch (woch) a device used to tell time that is worn or carried

water clock (wô′ tər kläk′) a clock that tells time by the amount of water that has dripped into a bowl

week (wēk) a unit of time that has seven days

winter (win′ tər) the time of year when the earth leans away from the sun

year (yir) a unit of time based on how long it takes the earth to go around the sun; 365 days

Bibliography

Binzen, Bill. *Year after Year.* New York:
    Coward, McCann and Geoghegan, Inc., 1976.

Claiborne, Robert, and Goudsmit, Samuel. *Time.*
    Morristown, N.J.: Silver Burdett Co., 1966.

Coleman, Lesley. *Book of Time.* Nashville, Tenn.:
    Thomas Nelson, Inc., 1971.

Kirst, Werner. *Time.* New York: Granada Publishing
    Inc., 1977.

White, William, Jr. *Cycle of the Seasons.* New York:
    Sterling Publishing Co., Inc., 1977.